ZOOM!

LOWER ELEMENTARY LEADER GUIDE

28 nineteen

KIDS

Each week we achieve our goal of reaching kids and their families for Christ by making programming for children Fun, Intentional, Scriptural, and Helpful.

Fun

The fun level of our activities should reflect the fun level of our God. 28nineteen™ KIDS teaches God's Word in a way that is attractive and memorable to the children. God is not boring, and neither are we! And, if children have a great time, they will want to return … with friends!

Intentional

We are intentional about knowing these children's names and needs. God hand-picked the children who attend your church every weekend. They are precious to Him and they are precious to us! The focus of 28nineteen™ KIDS is always on reaching children and their families for Jesus Christ.

Scriptural

28nineteen™ KIDS is an unapologetically Bible based curriculum. In other words, we stand on the Word of God. All of our Bible Study and Worship lessons come directly from the Bible and teach our children straight biblical truth.

Helpful

Our goal is to teach children to be "doers of the Word, and not merely hearers" (James 1:22). To do this, we teach practical applications of biblical truths in each lesson. The children should leave with a challenge or an action to live their lives for Christ.

TABLE OF CONTENTS

Lower Elementary Bible Study

MAIN POINT

The Bible is so rich! Every time we read a Bible story, be it the first or the fiftieth time, God can teach us something new. To help everyone stay on the same page, 28nineteen™ KIDS narrows in on one main point from the Bible story. Everything we do intentionally teaches the Bible story and this one point.

LEADER DEVOTION

The goal of the leader devotion is to help your leadership learn the lesson personally first. Secondly, our goal is to help your leadership feel an empowerment and excitement to share what they have learned with their classes. For this reason, each lesson begins with the same devotion for all leaders on an adult level. Background information, be it historical, cultural, or biblical, is incorporated to make the study richer in meaning for your leaders as well as for your kids. Additionally, the leader devotion helps your leadership team, be they Bible study teachers, worship leaders, or classroom helpers, to be on the same page.

ACTIVITIES

Actvities help kids stay engaged in the learning process while having fun. Each activity has a specific purpose and connects to the Bible lesson and main point for the day. Teachers can easily make this connection for themselves and their kids by reading the "Make the Connection" section below each activity.

- **Welcome Activities:** Many children find it difficult to walk into a group comfortably, thus it's helpful to have an activity that draws a child in and immediately gets them engaged. Welcome activities are designed to help all children feel they can confidently participate. These activities also serve as an introduction to the main point of the Bible lesson.

- **Crafts with Purpose:** 28nineteen™ KIDS does not have a craft for each lesson. Instead, crafts are included in lessons when they make sense and can be the most helpful to the kids as they learn.

- **Variety of Energy Levels:** Each lesson includes a variety of activities ranging in energy levels. Leaders can choose the activities that best fit the needs of their classes.

FAQ

This section is for you, leaders! Learning big truths often leads to big questions. If a child asks, we want you to be prepared.

BIBLE LESSON

Bible lessons are clearly outlined into four sections: Intro, Read the Bible, Present the Gospel, and Application.

 Intro: Short for "introduction," this section helps leaders grab kids' attention, quickly review past lessons, teach the overarching theme of the series, and get kids excited about the Bible story.

 Read the Bible: Now we get to the good stuff! In this section, leaders encourage kids to read in the Bible as they discover God's Word for themselves.

 Present the Gospel: The Bible is one big story, and it is all about Jesus! Each lesson seamlessly ties the Bible story to the truth of the Gospel. Leaders teach the truth of the Gospel and encourage kids to respond. Because we never know how many opportunities we will have to interact with each child, we never miss an opportunity to talk about Jesus.

 Application: Our goal is to teach children to be "doers of the Word, and not merely hearers" (James 1:22). To do this, we teach practical applications of biblical truths in each lesson. The children should leave with a challenge or an action to live their lives for Christ.

 Clues: Throughout the Bible lesson, kids read clues that direct them to the Bible.

MEMORY VERSE

The goal of the memory verse activities is long-term understanding and memorization of Scripture. For this reason, 28nineteen™ KIDS focuses on one verse or passage during each series. Throughout the series, kids are encouraged to memorize these verses in fun and interactive ways. Just like the activities, each memory verse section has a "Make the Connection" section to help teachers explain the meaning and practical applications of the verses kids are memorizing.

ZOOM PUZZLE

God has many characteristics and many names, but He is one God. To help kids visually understand this truth, we developed a puzzle. Kids take home pieces of the puzzle as they learn who God is. You can order these puzzles at 28nineteencurriculum.com.

ELOHIM:
God is Creator.

....

MEMORY VERSE

"Therefore, God elevated him to the place of highest honor and gave him the name above all other names, that at the name of Jesus every knee should bow, in heaven and on earth and under the earth, and every tongue declare that Jesus Christ is Lord, to the glory of God the Father." Philippians 2:9-11

ZOOM!

Bible Lesson: The Mystery of the World
(Genesis 1-2)

INVESTIGATIVE
SUPPLIES

ACTIVITY 1:

Art supplies, Memory verse sheet *(page 81)*

ACTIVITY 2:

Animal cards *(pages 83, 85, 87, 89, 91)*, Scissors, Music, Music player

BIBLE LESSON:

Clues *(page 93)*, Decoder (piece of red cellophane)

ACTIVITY 3:

Creation pictures *(pages 95, 97, 99)*, Balloons, Trash bags

ACTIVITY 4:

Modeling dough

ACTIVITY 5:

ELOHIM papers *(pages 101, 103)*, Music, Music player

LEADER DEVOTION

Read Genesis 1-2:3; Isaiah 40:28-31; Psalm 121:1-2; 139:13-14.

At first, the question "Who is God?" sounds simple; however, the more we think about it, the harder it becomes to answer. God is so many things. He is Creator. He is Provider. He is just and merciful and kind and loving. He is Father, and He is Friend. The list goes on and on. Our God is not only bigger than words can describe; He is bigger than our imaginations. Studying the individual names of God allows us to "zoom in" on a single aspect of God's character, breaking down the "Who is God?" question into more manageable concepts.

The first name of God in the Bible is "Elohim," God the Almighty Creator, and represents the plural Trinity of God the Father, God the Son, and God the Holy Spirit. Even this one name is packed full of information about our God. Throughout the Bible, God is praised for His work of creation. He made everything perfectly and on purpose, including you and me.

As you study the name Elohim and the fact that God is the Creator, you may want to do some things you may not normally do, such as spending time outside or looking up scientific facts and processes. Doing so will help you look at all of creation as God sees it – His. Every scientific law man has discovered was first created by God. Sir Isaac Newton, for all of his intellect, did not create gravity. Through the intelligence God created in him, he was able to discover God's creation. Copernicus, for all of his keen powers of observation, did not create a sun-centric universe. Elohim did and allowed Copernicus to discover a small piece of the system He put into place at the dawn of time.

The name Elohim reminds us we serve a God who is big enough and powerful enough to have created everything; yet, He is still involved in the small things. In Isaiah 40, God reminds us He is a source of strength to those who wait on Him. In Psalm 121, God reminds us He is not sleeping in our times of need. He is awake and aware. He is both the Creator and the Maintainer. In Psalm 139, God reminds us He knows us intimately – in such a small and detailed way, unexpected from One with such enormous power. God made us wonderfully.

Elohim is the Almighty Creator. He deserves our worship.

For more Bible study on Elohim, read Job 38-41; Isaiah 43:1-3, 7; Revelation 4:11.

WELCOME

ACTIVITY 1 • MEMORY VERSE

MATERIALS: Art supplies, Memory verse sheet *(page 81)*

DIRECTIONS: Tell kids to draw pictures around the words in Philippians 2:9 that will help them remember the verse and what it means. (Ex. Draw a "4" above the word "therefore" and a name tag above the word "name.") Work with kids to give them ideas if they need help.

MAKE THE CONNECTION:

During our new series, ZOOM, we are studying the different names of God. Philippians 2:9-11 tells us Jesus has the best name of all. Jesus deserves our worship, because Jesus is God. Many of you were very creative when drawing pictures for the words in the verses. Today we will learn the first name of God used in the Bible, Elohim, which means Creator. God is Creator!

ACTIVITY 2 • ANIMAL CARDS

MATERIALS: Animal cards *(pages 83, 85, 87, 89, 91)*, Scissors, Music, Music player

DIRECTIONS: Hand each person one animal card. Be sure to hand out an equal amount of heads, bodies, and legs. Have kids move around the room while you play the music. When the music stops, kids must form groups of three to make an animal with their cards (head, body, and a set of legs). When kids have gotten into groups, have them make up a name and a sound for that animal. Start the music and have the kids move around the room again. Play several times, so kids can make several silly animals!

MAKE THE CONNECTION:

- What was your favorite made-up animal?
- What was your favorite made-up animal noise?

God is very creative. Genesis 1-2 tells us He made all the different kinds of animals in just one day, and everything He made was good.

BIBLE LESSON

Before the Bible Lesson, hide clues 1-5 around the room *(page 93)*. Each clue relates to the Bible Lesson. Have kids scramble to find the clues before grabbing their Bibles and sitting down.

 INTRO

During our series, ZOOM, we will begin to answer the question "Who is God?" by ZOOMING in on the different names of God. The Bible gives God a lot of different names that all mean different things. Each name gives us a small clue to the big picture of who God is.

• How many names do you have? Do you have any nicknames?

You may not have any nicknames, but you definitely have more than one name. You are Son or Daughter to your parents. You are Brother or Sister to your siblings. At different times, you can be Helper, Athlete, Musician, or Friend. Those who have given their lives to Jesus have the name Christian.

Each of those names means something different. You are Son or Daughter, but that is not all you are. You are Friend, but that is not all you are, either. Each of these names ZOOMS in on one part of who you are as a person.

Today we are going to ZOOM in on the first name of God found in the Bible.

 Who has CLUE #1?

Give the person who found Clue #1 a "decoder" (a piece of red cellophane). Let them read the first clue to the class. Clue #1 reads, "Elohim is the first name of God found in the Bible."

The first name of God found in the Bible is Elohim (El-oh-heem). Where can we find this name of God in the Bible? I think we need another clue!

 Who has CLUE #2?

Give the person who found Clue #2 a "decoder" (a piece of red cellophane). Let them read the clue to the class. Clue #2 reads, "The Mystery of the World. Genesis 1:1."

 # READ THE BIBLE

Read Genesis 1:1.
In our Bibles, the word "Elohim" is translated in English as "God," because Elohim is one of the Hebrew names used for God. Elohim means "The All-Powerful Creator." God is the all-powerful Creator. Genesis 1-2 tells us the story of how God created the world in six days before resting on the seventh day.

On the first day, God created light. He looked at His creation and saw that it was good.

Genesis 1:6-8 tells us that on the second day, God created the sky. He separated the sky from the ocean, and saw that it was good.

On the third day, God created dry land and plants. When He was finished, He looked at everything He created and saw that it was good.

On the fourth day, God created the sun, moon, all of the planets, and the stars. God looked at all He had created and saw that ... you guessed it! It was good.

On the fifth day, God created every different kind of bird and every different kind of animal that lives in the sea. That is amazing! We are still discovering new sea creatures today! Our God is extremely creative and extremely powerful. God looked at all that He had created and saw that it was good.

On the sixth day, God created all of the different animals on the earth. God made giraffes, zebras, donkeys, alligators, dogs, cats, and more. Then God made something very special. God made people.

Read Genesis 1:26-28.
God made people differently than He made the animals. God made us to be in a

perfect relationship with Him. At the end of the sixth day, God looked at everything He had made and saw that it was very good.

 ## PRESENT THE GOSPEL

God made the world perfect. He created everything in perfect order. He created you and me to live in a perfect relationship, a friendship, with Him. Everything God made was good. But God did not want to force us to love Him. Instead, God gave us a choice: we could choose to love Him and obey Him, or we could choose to do things our own way, to sin. The Bible tells us in Romans 3:23 that every single person who has ever lived has sinned - except Jesus. The punishment for our sins, our wrong choices that go against God, is death and separation from God. When we sin, our perfect friendship with God is broken.

Thankfully, God loves us so much that He sent His only Son, Jesus, to take our punishment. Even though Jesus had never done anything wrong, He chose to die on the cross for all of the wrong choices you and I have made. After He died, Jesus came back to life three days later! Jesus is God, and because of Jesus we can be friends with God again.

ADMIT that you have sinned. BELIEVE Jesus is God's perfect Son who died on the cross for your sins and came back to life. CHOOSE to put Him in charge of your life from now on. Make Jesus the Lord, the Boss of everything you do, say, and think. Then God will create a clean heart in you, as you are forgiven for your sins and welcomed into a forever friendship with God! (Psalm 51:10)

 ## APPLICATION

God is Creator. It makes sense to see the name Elohim in the story of Creation. Where else does the Bible refer to God as the Almighty Creator?

 Who has CLUE #3?

Give the person who found Clue #3 a "decoder" (a piece of red cellophane). Let them read the clue to the class. Clue #3 reads, "Isaiah 40:28-31."

Read Isaiah 40:28-31.

God is strong. He is strong enough to create the entire world in only six days, and He is strong enough to help us. God, our Creator, deserves our worship.

 Who has CLUE #4?

Give the person who found Clue #4 a "decoder" (a piece of red cellophane). Let them read the clue to the class. Clue #4 reads, "Psalm 139:13-14."

Read Psalm 139:13-14.
God created you, and God created me. He loves us very much, and God does not make mistakes. God created you, and it was good. God, our Creator, deserves our worship.

 Who has CLUE #5?

Give the person who found Clue #5 a "decoder" (a piece of red cellophane). Let them read the clue to the class. Clue #5 reads, "Psalm 121:1-2."

Read Psalm 121:1-2.
The Creator of the universe is on our side, when we choose to put Him in charge. God, our Creator, deserves our worship.

PRAY

God is Creator.

ELOHIM

ACTIVITY 3 • CREATION CRAZINESS

MATERIALS: Creation pictures *(pages 95, 97, 99)*, Balloons, Trash bags

DIRECTIONS: *Before Class*, cut out three or four sets of Creation Pictures and put each picture inside a balloon. Blow up the balloons. Put each set of balloons in a trash bag.

During Class, review what God created on each day. Split your class into equal groups. Give each group a bag of balloons. Be sure there is at least one balloon for each child.

On your mark, kids must pop the balloons and work together to put the pictures in the order that God created each item. (Ex. A picture of plants should be put before a picture of the sun, etc.) Let groups use their Bibles to help them with the order. When all pictures have been put in the correct order, teams must lie down on the ground to "rest". The first team to rest wins.

 MAKE THE CONNECTION:

God created a lot in six days.
- Why do you think God created light and color?
- Why do you think God created plants and animals?
- What is your favorite thing that God created? Why?

God created everything on purpose and for a purpose. Everything God created was good. He made everything PERFECTLY! Let's take some time, right now, to worship God and thank Him for our favorite things He created.

LEAD YOUR CLASS IN PRAYER. Tell the kids you are going to pray, leaving a silent space for them to complete the sentences to God themselves, in silent prayer.

(For example, "Dear God, I love that You created _____. I think You are great because _____. Thank You for _____.")

ACTIVITY 4 • CREATION STATION

MATERIALS: Modeling dough

DIRECTIONS: Hand each person a small amount of modeling dough. Have your kids mold their dough into one of their favorite things God created. As time allows, let kids mold the dough into another favorite thing God created.

MAKE THE CONNECTION:

• What is your favorite thing God created and why?

God created so many good things. God is Elohim, the Almighty Creator. He made everything just by speaking. God is amazing and deserves our worship - the focus of our hearts.

ACTIVITY 5 • SPELL IT OUT: ELOHIM

MATERIALS: ELOHIM papers *(pages 101, 103)*, Music, Music player

DIRECTIONS: Hand one paper to each player. If your group does not evenly split into groups of six, give some players two consecutive letters. Play music. Have kids walk around the room until the music stops. When the music stops, kids must get in groups of six to spell out the name "Elohim." When everyone has found a group, have the group state the meaning of the name "Elohim" and one thing God created. Start the music again. Have kids get in different groups each time you stop the music.

MAKE THE CONNECTION:

Who is God? God is many things, and all of them are good. Today, we ZOOMED in on Elohim, the name of God that tells us God is the Almighty Creator. Everything God made was good and perfect.

• What does that tell you about God?
• Does God make mistakes?
• Is God creative?
• Is God powerful?

Our God is amazing, and that is just the first name of God. It is only one small piece of who God is. Each name gives us a small clue to the big picture of who God is.

Q: Aren't there a lot of theories about how the world was made?

A: Yes there are, and we are not going to go into that right now. The bottom line is those theories are just that - theories, guesses. In here, we are going to stick to the facts. The facts are God was there when He created the world, not us. We will teach what is in the Bible, because the Bible is God's Word.

Q: Are we like animals?

A: Yes and no. Our bodies function a lot like animals' bodies, but God made us differently. Genesis 1:26 says God made us in His image. He made us to have a relationship with Him. God made people special and loves us very much.

EL SHADDAI:
God is Enough.

MEMORY VERSE

"Therefore, God elevated him to the place of highest honor and gave him the name above all other names, that at the name of Jesus every knee should bow, in heaven and on earth and under the earth, and every tongue declare that Jesus Christ is Lord, to the glory of God the Father." Philippians 2:9-11

ZOOM!

Bible Lesson: The Mystery of the Promise
(Genesis 17:1-8)

INVESTIGATIVE
SUPPLIES

ACTIVITY 1:

Baby name book

ACTIVITY 2:

None

BIBLE LESSON:

Clues *(page 105)*, Decoder (piece of red cellophane)

ACTIVITY 3:

Paper strips, Marker

ACTIVITY 4:

White board, Dry erase markers, Worship music, Music player

ACTIVITY 5:

EL SHADDAI papers *(pages 107, 109, 111)*, Music, Music player

LEADER DEVOTION

Read Genesis 17:1-8, 17-19; 18:13-14.

God made a seemingly impossible promise to Abram before changing his name to Abraham. "Abram" means "exalted father," and "Abraham" means "father of many nations." Try to put yourself in ninety-nine year old Abram's shoes. For ninety-nine years, his name meant he would be an exalted father; yet, here he was, childless in his old age. God gave Abram a new name, a new identity as a father of many nations, that required implicit faith in His ability to do all that He had promised. Both Abram and Sarai laughed when they heard God's promise.

In fact, Genesis 17 is not the first time God told Abram he would be a father of many. In Genesis 12, God promises, "I will make you a great nation…" Confused, Sarai convinced her husband she was not enough. Surely, God did not mean Abram would have children by her. She was only ten years younger than Abram and thought it was impossible for a woman like her to have children. Genesis 16 tells us Abram and Sarai foolishly tried to fulfill God's promise for Him. Hagar gave birth to Ishmael. While God did promise to bless Ishmael, Ishmael was not a part of God's original promise.

Abram and Sarai were not enough to accomplish such a seemingly impossible promise on God's behalf, and they did not need to be. They acted outside of His timing and outside of His will, because they did not yet understand God is El Shaddai, the All-Sufficient One. He is strong enough to accomplish all He has promised in the way He has promised. He does not ask us to be enough. El Shaddai is enough.

In the New Testament, Jesus proves He is also God Almighty, the All Sufficient One. On the cross, Jesus took the punishment for the sins of the world. He paid for our sins in full, and His resurrection proves that His payment was enough. (Rom. 6:10, Heb. 10:12-14)

Whatever you are facing today, God is enough. He is strong enough. He is wise enough. He is loving enough. He is present enough. (2 Cor. 12:9-10) The Almighty God, the El Shaddai, is enough. Therefore, perhaps impossible is a word we Christians should erase from our vocabulary. If we truly claim to serve the Almighty, the All-Sufficient One, the El Shaddai, then nothing is impossible. God has proven over and over again that nothing is impossible for Him. Will you let go of the effort to be enough for everyone and everything and instead trust Him to be enough for you?

WELCOME

ACTIVITY 1 • MEMORY VERSE

MATERIALS: Baby name book

DIRECTIONS: Review Philippians 2:9 together. Make motions that remind you of the meaning of the words in the verse. As you have time, find out what kids' names mean using a baby name book.

MAKE THE CONNECTION:

- Do you know what your name means?

Philippians 2:9 tells us Jesus earned a name that is much better than anyone else's name, when He died on the cross to take the punishment for our sins and came back to life three days later. God is amazing! Studying His many names is one way we can ZOOM in to learn who God is.

ACTIVITY 2 • IMPOSSIBLE OR NOT?

MATERIALS: None

DIRECTIONS: Challenge your class to accomplish several of the "impossible" tasks below.

1. Lick your elbow.
2. Join hands. Try to make different shapes like a rectangle, star, etc. with your eyes closed.
3. Jump from one side of the room to the other side in a single jump.
4. Rub your stomach and pat your head while singing "Mary Had a Little Lamb."
5. Twiddle your thumbs in different directions. (One clockwise, the other counter-clockwise.)

MAKE THE CONNECTION:

Those challenges were difficult. Some of them were even impossible! Today we are going to learn that nothing is impossible with God. He is able to do what He says He can do. He is strong enough, smart enough, and loving enough to do anything. No matter what is going on, God is enough.

BIBLE LESSON

Before the Bible Lesson, hide clues 1-5 around the room *(page 105)*. Each clue relates to the Bible Lesson. Have kids scramble to find the clues before grabbing their Bibles and sitting down.

 INTRO

Remember, during ZOOM, we will answer the question "Who is God?" by ZOOMING in on the different names of God. The Bible gives God a lot of different names that all mean different things. Each name gives us a small clue to the big picture of who God is. Last week, we learned that God is Elohim. Does anyone remember what that name of God means? "Elohim" means "Almighty Creator." God is our Creator!

Today we are going to ZOOM in on another one of God's names.

 Who has CLUE #1?

Give the person who found Clue #1 a "decoder" (a piece of red cellophane). Let them read the first clue to the class. Clue #1 reads, "'El Shaddai' means 'God Almighty, the All-Sufficient One.'" (Ell - SHAD - eye)

- Everyone say "El Shaddai" with me. *(Ell - SHAD - eye)*
- Does anyone know what "sufficient" means? Sufficient means "enough," so the name "El Shaddai" reminds us that God is enough.

 READ THE BIBLE

Let's look in the Bible for clues. Where does God first use the name "El Shaddai?"

Who has CLUE #2?

Give the person who found Clue #2 a "decoder" (a piece of red cellophane). Let them read the clue to the class. Clue #2 reads, "The Mystery of the Promise. Genesis 17:1-8."

What promise? Let's follow the clues and find out. **Read Genesis 17:1-8.**

Remember, "El Shaddai" is a Hebrew name for God. In verse one of our English Bibles, this name of God is translated as "God Almighty."

- How old was Abram at this time? *(99 years old)*
- What did God promise Abram / Abraham? *(God promised to make him a father of nations and give him the land of Caanan.)*

 Who has CLUE #3?

Give the person who found Clue #3 a "decoder" (a piece of red cellophane). Let them read the clue to the class. Clue #3 reads, "The name 'Abram' means 'exalted father.'"

Today the meaning of our names is not always important. It is fun to know what your name means, but it doesn't usually mean anything about the kind of person you are. In Bible times, though, names were supposed to mean something important about who you were. Abram was not a father, but his name meant "exalted father." Abram was probably very sad about this.

 Who has CLUE #4?

Give the person who found Clue #4 a "decoder" (a piece of red cellophane). Let them read the clue to the class. Clue #4 reads, "The name 'Abraham' means 'father of many nations.'"

- What do you need to be a father, especially a father of many nations? *(a child)*

This is not the first time God had promised Abram he would be a father to a nation. Genesis 12 tells us he was 75 years old the first time God made the same promise. Abram had waited a long time, but God's promise had not changed.

Read Genesis 17:17-21.
Abram did not believe that God was going to give him a son through Sarai, his wife. Abram really wanted to be a father. He really wanted God's promise to come true,

but he did not think God could do everything He said He could do. Abram and Sarai decided Abram should have a baby with another woman in order to make God's promise come true.

God blessed the little baby, Ishmael, but said that Ishmael was not the son God promised to Abram. God introduced Himself to Abram as "El Shaddai" to teach Abram He is enough. God can do everything He says He can do. Nothing is impossible for God.

Read Genesis 18:13-14.
Sarah could not believe it, but God told Abraham once again that He was enough. God could keep His promise even if it sounded impossible to Abraham and Sarah. Genesis 21 tells us God kept His promise. Sarah gave birth to a baby boy named Isaac. Sarah was ninety years old!

Boys and girls, God kept His promise to Abraham and Sarah. He was strong enough to do everything He said He would do. God is enough!

 # PRESENT THE GOSPEL

 Who has CLUE #5?

Give the person who found Clue #5 a "decoder" (a piece of red cellophane). Let them read the clue to the class. Clue #5 reads, "Jesus is enough."

Jesus is enough for us, too. The Bible says we all have done wrong; we all have sinned against God. The punishment for our sin is death and separation from God. There is nothing we can do to fix our sins. No amount of good things we do will ever be enough. Thankfully, God is enough, and He loves us very, very much. Jesus came to earth and lived a perfect life, a life without any sin. Then Jesus chose to die on the cross to take the punishment we deserve for the wrong choices we have made. Jesus, the perfect Son of God, took our punishment for us. After Jesus had been dead for three days, He came back to life! Jesus' payment for our sins on the cross was, and is, enough for us.

ADMIT you have done wrong things. Tell God you know your wrong choices are your fault. Tell God you are sorry; then tell Him you believe in Jesus. BELIEVE He really is God, and He really took your punishment for you when He chose to die on the cross for your sins. Thank Him that His sacrifice on the cross was enough for you. CHOOSE to make Jesus in charge of your life. Make Jesus your Lord, your Boss, from now on.

Jesus' payment for our sins was enough for us to be forgiven and accepted into God's heavenly family. That is amazing!

 APPLICATION

Luke 1:37 says, "For the word of God will never fail."

Matthew 19:26 says, "Jesus looked at them intently and said, 'Humanly speaking, it is impossible. But with God everything is possible.'"

Jeremiah 32:27 says, "I am the LORD, the God of all the peoples of the world. Is anything too hard for me?"

Nothing is impossible for God, our El Shaddai. He can handle any problem we might have. God is enough, so we can trust Him with everything.

PRAY

God is Enough. EL SHADDAI

ACTIVITY 3 • WHAT YOU REALLY NEED

MATERIALS: Paper strips, Marker

DIRECTIONS: Write numbers 1-30 on paper strips. Each round lasts ten seconds. (To make the game more difficult, add more numbers. To play with multiple people at the same time, hide as many of the special number around the room as you have players.)

Round 1: Send the contestant out of the room while other students place numbers 1-10 face down around the room. When the contestant enters, tell them that finding #7 is what they need to advance to the next round.

Round 2: Send the contestant out of the room while other students place numbers 1-20 face down around the room. When the contestant enters, tell them that finding #18 is what they need to advance to the next round.

Round 3: Send the contestant out of the room while other students place numbers 1-30 face down around the room. When the contestant enters, tell them that finding #22 is what they need to advance to the next round.

MAKE THE CONNECTION:
- In Round 1, finding #7 was enough. If you found numbers 3, 8, and 5, would you have advanced to the next level? Why not?
- Did it matter how many numbers you collected in this game? Explain your answer.

To advance to the next round, you had to find the correct number. Finding that number was all you really needed to win the game.

- What do we need in life? *(food, clothes, family, etc.)*
- What is the one thing we need more than anything else?
- Luke 18-19 tells us about a Rich Young Ruler and Zaccheus. Zaccheus gave up his money and followed Jesus, but the Rich Young Ruler did not think having Jesus in his life was enough. He wanted to have money, too. Is Jesus "enough?" Explain your answer.

God's name, "El Shaddai," means that God is enough. He is all we really need.

ACTIVITY 4 • WORSHIP MOMENT

MATERIALS: White board, Dry erase markers, Worship music, Music player

DIRECTIONS: Set the tone for this activity by explaining you are about to do something that worships God by focusing on the great things He has done.

Let kids take turns going to the board to write examples of the amazing things God has done that remind us that nothing is impossible for God. Have kids write one thing at a time. Allow kids to get back in line if they remember another amazing story of what God can do.

When they have finished, read the examples the kids have written on the board. End the time with prayer.

MAKE THE CONNECTION:

Nothing is impossible with God! He is strong enough, smart enough, good enough, loving enough, and faithful enough to do everything He says He can do. Our God, El Shaddai, is enough!

Read 2 Corinthians 12:9-10.

Even when we feel our weakest, God is strong. We can trust that He can handle whatever comes our way.

He gave Abraham a son.

He helped Joshua defeat Jericho.

He gave the disciples the power to heal people.

Jesus came back to life.

Jesus calmed the storm.

He parted the Red Sea.

He helped David defeat Goliath.

He saved Daniel from the lion's den.

ACTIVITY 5 • SPELL IT OUT: EL SHADDAI

MATERIALS: EL SHADDAI papers *(pages 107, 109, 111)*, Music, Music player

DIRECTIONS: Hand one paper to each player. If your group does not evenly split into groups of nine, give some players two consecutive letters. Play music. Have kids walk around the room until the music stops. When the music stops, kids must get in groups of nine to spell out the name "El Shaddai." When everyone has found a group, have the group state the meaning of the name "El Shaddai" and one "impossible" thing God has done (i.e. parting the Red Sea, coming back to life, calming the storm, etc.). Start the music again. Have kids get in different groups each time you stop the music.

MAKE THE CONNECTION:

Who is God? God is many things, and all of them are good! Today we ZOOMED in on "El Shaddai," the name of God that tells us God is the All Sufficient One! God is enough. He is strong enough. He is smart enough. He is loving enough.

- What does that tell you about God?
- Is anything impossible for God?
- Is there any problem God can't fix?
- Do you need anything besides God in life?

Nothing is impossible with God! No matter what problem you face, God is enough. He is all we need.

Q: Why did God wait so long to give Abraham a son?

A: God promised Abraham He would use him as a blessing to everyone in the world. God used Abraham and his family as an object lesson to the people. God wanted everyone to know that Isaac's birth was a miracle that only God could do. Can you think of another miracle birth? Jesus! Isaac's birth was a picture of Jesus, God's plan to save the world from sin.

Q: Isn't "El Shaddai" a song?

A: Yes! Made popular by Amy Grant, "El Shaddai" is a praise song about God's plan to save the world from sin. The song uses a few Hebrew words as well. The English phrases immediately after the Hebrew phrases basically translate the Hebrew words.

CLUE 3

JEHOVAH-JIREH: God is Provider.

. . . .

MEMORY VERSE

"Therefore, God elevated him to the place of highest honor and gave him the name above all other names, that at the name of Jesus every knee should bow, in heaven and on earth and under the earth, and every tongue declare that Jesus Christ is Lord, to the glory of God the Father." Philippians 2:9-11

ZOOM!

Bible Lesson: The Mystery of the Ram

(Genesis 22:1-19)

INVESTIGATIVE
SUPPLIES

ACTIVITY 1:

Jehovah-Jireh color by number page *(page 113)*,
Colors

ACTIVITY 2:

Blindfolds, Ping pong balls, Hula hoops,
Butcher paper, Markers

BIBLE LESSON:

Clues *(page 115)*, Decoder (piece of red cellophane)

ACTIVITY 3:

None

ACTIVITY 4:

Paper, Markers, Chairs (or other targets)

ACTIVITY 5:

JEHOVAH-JIREH papers *(pages 117, 119)*, Music, Music player

ZOOM!

LEADER DEVOTION

Read Genesis 22:1-19.

The story of Abraham's "almost" sacrifice of his son, Isaac, is a hard story to take. Why would God ask Abraham to give up his God-given gift? Why, knowing how important fatherhood was to him, would God test Abraham in this way? How was Abraham able to obey God without even a hint of questioning or arguing?

While we know the end of the story, that God never intended for Abraham to commit a human sacrifice, Abraham must have had extraordinary faith in God to obey. Theologians posit Abraham believed God would raise his son from the dead. He had seen God do a miracle in the birth of his son, Isaac, and he believed God was able to do even more. Still, our hearts go out to Abraham, when his innocent son looks to his father and asks, **"Where is the lamb for the burnt offering?"** while carrying the wood for his sacrifice on his own back. In faith, Abraham replied, **"God will provide for Himself the lamb for the burnt offering, my son."**

Mount Moriah, the place Abraham named "The Lord Will Provide," later became the location of Solomon's temple and consequently the location of Israel's sacrifices to the Lord. Every time a sacrifice was made, it was made on the promise that the Lord will provide. The sacrifices were made in the same place, where God ultimately did not ask Abraham to give up his only son, but where He Himself provided the ram that would take Isaac's place. God knows the pain of sacrificing His only Son. Jesus, God's only Son, also carried the wood on His back to Calvary. Jesus was obedient even to death on a cross, where He died a sacrificial lamb, paying for the sins of the world once and for all. God will provide.

Though that would be enough, God also provides for our daily needs. In *Lord, I Want to Know You*, Kay Arthur states, "He is a God who is for you, not against you. In any test, you can lay your Isaac on the altar. You can worship Jehovah-jireh in obedience and know that whatever you need, the Lord will provide it."

What is your "Isaac?" We do not need to hold on to anything more tightly than the Lord. God is on our side; therefore, we have no need to worry, no need to fear. Though we may not see how God will provide or understand His plan, we can know, beyond a shadow of a doubt, He will take care of us. His name is Jehovah-Jireh.

For more on God's provision, read
Matt. 6:25-34; Lk. 11:1-13;
Rom. 8:28-37; Phil. 4:10-19.

WELCOME

ACTIVITY 1 • COLOR BY NUMBER

MATERIALS: Jehovah-Jireh color by number page *(page 113)*, Colors

DIRECTIONS: Tell kids to answer the question, "What name of God means 'God is Provider?'" by coloring the numbers on the page. When kids have found the answer, make the connection. Let them finish coloring as time allows.

MAKE THE CONNECTION:

Did anyone have trouble seeing the name "Jehovah-Jireh" at first? You may or may not have been able to see the name at first, but it was always there. In the same way, we cannot always see how God will provide for us, but we can trust He is always there. God is our Provider. He will take care of what we really need for all eternity, when we choose to trust in Him.

ACTIVITY 2 • TRUST AND OBEY

MATERIALS: Blindfolds, Ping pong balls, Hula hoops, Butcher paper, Markers

DIRECTIONS: Set up a relay activity. Choose co-leaders, or kids with leadership abilities, to guide contestants in each corner. Have everyone else pair off. During the game, one person in each pair is blindfolded, while the other leads them to each corner. No one can touch the blindfolded partner during this game. Be sure everyone gets a chance to be blindfolded.

Corner 1: Throw a ping pong ball into the target zone. (Tape off a fairly large target zone.)
Corner 2: Walk through the hula hoops without touching them.
Corner 3: Draw a smiley face on the paper.
Corner 4: Sit in a taped-off target zone.

MAKE THE CONNECTION:

When you were blindfolded, you had to trust your partners and your game leaders to lead you where you needed to go and give you what you needed to complete each game. In today's Bible story, Abraham obeyed God and trusted Him to provide for him and his family.

BIBLE LESSON

Before the Bible Lesson, hide clues 1-5 around the room *(page 115)*. Each clue relates to the Bible Lesson. Have kids scramble to find the clues before grabbing their Bibles and sitting down.

 INTRO

During ZOOM, we are beginning to answer the question "Who is God?" by ZOOMING in on different names of God. The Bible gives God a lot of different names that all mean different things, and each name gives us a small clue to the big picture of who God is. We learned God is Elohim, our Creator. We learned God is El Shaddai, the All Sufficient One. God is enough. Nothing is impossible for God!

Today we are going to ZOOM in on another one of God's names.

 Who has CLUE #1?

Give the person who found Clue #1 a "decoder" (a piece of red cellophane). Let them read the first clue to the class. Clue #1 reads, "'Jehovah-Jireh' means 'God is Provider.'" (Ji-hoh-vuh - Ji-ra)

A provider gives someone what they need. For example, your parents provide, or give, many things to you.

- What are a few ways your parents provide for you?
- Today our main point is God is Provider. What are a few ways God provides for you?

God provides for us in a lot of ways. There are too many ways to count. Today we are going to ZOOM in on one MAJOR way God provides for us. I wonder where we should look in the Bible for God's name, Jehovah-Jireh.

 Who has CLUE #2?

Give the person who found Clue #2 a "decoder" (a piece of red cellophane). Let them read the clue to the class. Clue #2 reads, "Genesis 22: The Mystery of the Ram."

 # READ THE BIBLE

Oh good! Genesis 22 is amazing! We are going to need a little background before we start this story. Last week we learned God promised a son to Abraham and his wife, Sarah. Although it seemed impossible for them to have a child in their old age, God kept His promise. Sarah gave birth to a baby boy named Isaac. Isaac was Abraham and Sarah's miracle son.

Now fast forward a little in your mind. In Genesis 22, which we are about to read together, Isaac was not a baby anymore. I think we still need one more clue before we study this true story from the Bible.

 Who has CLUE #3?

Give the person who found Clue #3 a "decoder" (a piece of red cellophane). Let them read the clue to the class. Clue #3 reads, "In the Old Testament, the death of an innocent animal during a sacrifice covered over the sins of the people."

That's right. The punishment for sin is death and separation from God. God loves us very much and wants to have a friendship with us. He set up a system for people to cover over their sins until He would send a Savior, who would clean the sin from their hearts and ours once and for all. God set up a system where an innocent animal could take the punishment for the people's sins, but the payment was never enough. People kept sinning and needing to make sacrifices to God to cover over their sins.

Now I think we have enough clues to understand the Bible story for today.

Read Genesis 22:1-2.

- What did God tell Abraham to do?
- How do you think Abraham felt about God's instructions?

God had told Abraham He was going to bless the world through him. Abraham loved Isaac very much, and he trusted God had a plan. Abraham had seen God do a miracle when his son was born. He knew he could trust God now, too. Abraham decided to obey God. He packed the things he needed for the sacrifice and took Isaac on the three-day journey to the mountain.

Read Genesis 22:4-5.
Abraham told his servants that both he and Isaac would come back. Abraham trusted that God had a plan, even if he did not yet know what His plan was.

Read Genesis 22:6-8.
Isaac noticed they did not have a lamb for the sacrifice. He did not yet know that God had instructed Abraham to sacrifice Isaac. Abraham continued up the mountain with Isaac. He told his son God would provide the lamb.

Abraham trusted that God would take care of everything, even though he did not know how God was going to provide. Maybe God would provide a lamb. Or maybe God would bring Isaac back to life. Abraham didn't know, but he kept going up the mountain. He kept choosing to trust and obey, even when it was not an easy thing to do.

Read Genesis 22:9-13.
Isaac was old enough to fight off his aging father, but he let Abraham tie him up and place him on the altar. Isaac trusted his father, and his father trusted God. Right before Abraham brought the knife down, an angel stopped him. God never intended for Isaac to get hurt. God had everything under control the whole time. Abraham had proven he loved God more than anything else in his life, even his only son.

Read Genesis 22:13-14.
God provided! God provided a ram for the sacrifice to take Isaac's place. Abraham was right to obey God and trust Him. Abraham renamed the mountain Jehovah-Jireh, "The LORD Will Provide," and worshiped God with his son, Isaac, on the mountain top.

PRESENT THE GOSPEL

God told Abraham to sacrifice Isaac, because He wanted to give us a picture of His only Son, Jesus. In the end, Abraham did not have to give up his only son, but God did give up His only Son, Jesus. Jesus, God's Son, came to earth and lived a perfect life. He was innocent. Then Jesus chose to be like the innocent lambs that were sacrificed. He took the punishment for our sins, when He died on the cross.

 Who has CLUE #4?

Give the person who found Clue #4 a "decoder" (a piece of red cellophane). Let them read the clue to the class. Clue #4 reads, "Jesus is 100% God and 100% man."

That's right. Jesus was 100% God and 100% man, so His payment for our sin was much better than an animal sacrifice. Jesus' payment was enough. Jesus came back to life three days later, so everyone would know His payment was enough. No one needs animals to cover up their sins ever again. Jesus did much more than cover them up. Jesus wiped away our sins forever.

Now because God provided Jesus' sacrifice, our hearts can be clean of sin. Every wrong choice you and I have made can be forgiven, because Jesus has already taken our punishment. The Bible says in **Romans 10:9, "That if you confess with your mouth, Jesus as Lord, and believe in your heart that God raised Him from the dead, you will be saved."** Tell God you are sorry for the sins, the wrong choices, you have made. Tell Him you believe with your whole heart that Jesus' payment for your sins on the cross was enough. Tell Him you believe Jesus came back to life three days later. Then choose to put Jesus in charge of your life. Make Jesus your Boss. God has provided a way for us to be saved! Because of Jesus, we can be a part of God's forever family. That is Good News!

 # APPLICATION

God provided a ram to take Isaac's place on the altar. Abraham trusted and obeyed God, and God provided. God provides for us, too. He has already provided a way for us to live in Heaven with Him forever through His only Son, Jesus. That is amazing.

God provides for us in many ways.

? Who has CLUE #5?

Give the person who found Clue #5 a "decoder" (a piece of red cellophane). Let them read the clue to the class. Clue #5 reads, "Matthew 6:31-34."

Read Matthew 6:31-34.

God knows what we need. We can trust Him to take care of us. We may not always understand how God will take care of us. We may not always understand God's plan for our lives. But like Abraham, we can always trust and obey God. God is our Jehovah-Jireh, our Provider.

PRAY

Pray with your class. Let kids take turns thanking God for giving them what they need or lead a silent prayer of thanks to God.

ACTIVITY 3 • SUBSTITUTION FREEZE TAG

MATERIALS: None

DIRECTIONS: In this version of freeze tag, "it" freezes someone by tagging them. In order to "unfreeze" someone, allowing them to play again, you must "freeze" in that person's place. Play several short games with different people playing as "it" each time.

MAKE THE CONNECTION:

A substitute is someone who takes the place of someone else. In school, a substitute teacher takes the place of your regular teacher. In sports, a substitute player takes the place of a tired or injured player.

- What substitute did God provide for Abraham's son, Isaac, on Mount Moriah?
- What substitute did God provide for us? In other words, who took our place? Who took the punishment that we deserved for our sin?

In our game of freeze tag, you gave up your ability to play the game, so other people could play. Jesus gave up His life, so we could live forever in Heaven with Him. Jesus provided the way for us to be with Him. That is amazing!

ACTIVITY 4 • MEMORY VERSE

MATERIALS: Paper, Markers, Chairs (or other targets)

DIRECTIONS: *Before Class*, write Philippians 2:9-10, one word at a time, on squares of paper. Make as many sets of the verse as you will have teams.

During Class, review Philippians 2:9. Read Philippians 2:10 together several times. Then split your class into teams. Have each team line up opposite a chair or other target. Distribute the verse papers among the members of each team. On your mark, teams wad up the verse papers and race to throw them at the target. Once the paper wad has successfully hit the target, team members can unfold the paper and begin to put the verse in order. If a player misses the target, they can try again until they or another member of the team hits the target. The first team to correctly assemble the verses wins!

MAKE THE CONNECTION:

You did a great job hitting the target. Sometimes the paper went over the target. Sometimes the paper went under the target, and sometimes the paper landed right on the target. The second part of our memory verse for this series tells us one day everyone will understand that Jesus is Lord. When they hear His Name, everyone above the earth (followers of Jesus who have died and are now living in Heaven), on the earth, and under the earth (people who did not choose to follow Jesus, who have died, and who are now living without God in a real place called Hell) will bow to Him.

Let's not wait to worship Jesus! Let's worship Him right now. Can you think of names of Jesus? (Let kids call out names like Savior, Friend, Lord, etc. before closing in prayer.)

ACTIVITY 5 • SPELL IT OUT: JEHOVAH-JIREH

MATERIALS: JEHOVAH-JIREH papers *(pages 117, 119)*, Music, Music player

DIRECTIONS: Hand one paper to each player. If your group does not evenly split into groups of six, give some players two consecutive letters. Play music. Have kids walk around the room until the music stops. When the music stops, kids must get in groups of six to spell out the name "Jehovah-Jireh." When everyone has found a group, have the group state the meaning of the name "Jehovah-Jireh" and one thing God has provided for them. Start the music again. Have kids get in different groups each time you stop the music.

MAKE THE CONNECTION:

Who is God? God is many things, and all of them are good. Today we ZOOMED in on Jehovah-Jireh, the name of God that tells us God is our Provider. God knows what we need. He is willing and able to take care of us for all eternity.

- What does this tell you about God?
- What has God provided for you?
- How has Jesus provided for us? (HINT: How is Jesus like the ram in Genesis 22?)

God knows what we really need. That's why He sent His Son, Jesus, to take our place on the cross. God is our Provider.

FAQ

Q: Will God ask my parents to sacrifice me?

A: No! God used Abraham and his family to be a blessing for the whole world. He used Abraham and Isaac as an object lesson, a picture, of how He planned to save the world from sin. Remember, God did not make Abraham give up his only son. God did give up His only Son, Jesus. God will not ask your parents to sacrifice you, because Jesus has already come. God's plans are good. Aren't you glad you have a God who provides for you? I know I am.

Q: If God is our provider, why are there poor people?

A: God does provide for our needs here on earth, but He is much more concerned about our eternity. God provided a way for us to get to Heaven, so we can spend forever in Heaven with Him. We may not always understand why God does what He does, and that is okay. God knows what He is doing. He has a plan, and even though we may not know how He will provide, we can trust that He will. (For further study, read Philippians 4:11-13.)

CLUE 4

YAHWEH:
God is I AM.

....

MEMORY VERSE

"Therefore, God elevated him to the place of highest honor and gave him the name above all other names, that at the name of Jesus every knee should bow, in heaven and on earth and under the earth, and every tongue declare that Jesus Christ is Lord, to the glory of God the Father." Philippians 2:9-11

ZO?M!

Bible Lesson: The Mystery of the Name
(Exodus 3-4:13)

INVESTIGATIVE
SUPPLIES

ACTIVITY 1:

Burning bush color sheet *(pages 121)*, Crayons,
Watercolor paint, Paintbrushes, Straws

ACTIVITY 2:

Fact or Fiction cards *(pages 123, 125)*, Bandanna, Bean bag, Bucket

BIBLE LESSON:

Clues *(page 127)*, Decoder (piece of red cellophane)

ACTIVITY 3:

Paper hole punch confetti, Cups, Marker

ACTIVITY 4:

Balloons, Balloon pumps, Small paper strips, Pen, Painters' tape
Alternate Memory Verse Game: Wind-up toys

ACTIVITY 5:

YAHWEH papers *(pages 129, 131)*, Music, Music player

LEADER DEVOTION

Read Exodus 3-4.

Until God introduces Himself as Yahweh, Moses refers to Him as Elohim, a more general name for God as the Creator. In Egypt, Moses grew up in an environment where many gods were worshiped, and he likely did not have an intimate knowledge of God. Though he identified himself with the Hebrew people, Moses had a confusing heritage. He was raised as a prince of Egypt, but he saw the injustice of his kinsmen's slavery to Pharaoh. He knew the comfort of living in the palace but felt the pain of his people's forced labor.

In anger, Moses had once tried to right the wrongs done to his people. In Exodus 2:11-15, Moses kills an Egyptian task master who was beating a Hebrew slave. His failure caused him to run to Midian. When God spoke to Moses through the burning bush, Moses wanted and needed clarification. Pharaoh thought himself a god. Who was Moses to say gave him such bold orders? Which god was he supposed to say put him in charge of the Hebrews, the people he deserted almost forty years ago? Moses must have wondered how this time would be different from the first. God responds to the fear behind Moses' question with His name, "I AM WHO I AM." God will be behind Moses. The one true God, the only living God, the self-existent One, is sending Moses to set His people free.

Still Moses was concerned he was not enough. He knew he was not qualified for the job. God was patient with Moses, answering his every objection with the assurance that I AM would be with him every step of the way. The first time, Moses acted alone and out of anger. This time, Moses would act with the power of God on his side and the assurance that God could do everything He said He could do.

The names Yahweh and Jehovah both stem from the same Hebrew root word "havah," the verb meaning "to be." God is the Self-Existent One. He is the Alpha and the Omega, the unchanging One. Yahweh is God regardless of circumstance, culture, or popular opinion. God chose to include Moses as an important part of His plan to free the Hebrews, but He did not need Moses to free His people. Moses, as insufficient as he felt, was incapable of messing up God's plans, because God is I AM. Yahweh will accomplish His plans; we are simply to trust Him and enjoy being a part of what He is doing on this earth.

Do you identify with Moses? Do you feel ill-equipped for the challenges God has placed before you? Take heart. Our God is patient with us, and He is with us. He is unchangeable, and His ways are good. Like Moses, draw close to God, and watch what the Great I AM will do through you.

WELCOME

ACTIVITY 1 • BURNING BUSH PAINTING

MATERIALS: Burning bush color sheet *(page 121)*, Crayons, Watercolor paint, Paintbrushes, Straws

DIRECTIONS: Have kids color the burning bush color sheet with crayons. Then have kids blot watery splotches of red, yellow, and orange paint on top of the bush. Quickly have them blow the paint around with a straw to make the paint look like flames.

MAKE THE CONNECTION:

Your paintings look amazing! The watercolor makes the bush look like it's on fire, but your leaves are still green. The Bible tells us in Exodus 3 that Moses saw something very similar in the desert. He saw a bush that was on fire, but all of its leaves were still green. The bush was not burning away. God used the bush to talk to Moses. Isn't God amazing?

ACTIVITY 2 • FACT OR FICTION

MATERIALS: Fact or Fiction cards *(pages 123, 125)*, Bandanna, Bean bag, Bucket

DIRECTIONS: Divide your class into two teams. Place a bandanna in the center of the room, and choose a contestant from each team. As soon as you finish reading the card, the first contestant to grab the bandanna gets to answer either "fact" or "fiction." If they answer correctly, their team wins 1,000 points. The team who has the most points at the end of the game wins. (For added fun, give 500 bonus points to contestants who can toss a bean bag into a bucket. This may help a losing team get back into the game.)

MAKE THE CONNECTION:

Moses needed to know God was real, unlike the many other gods worshiped in Egypt, where he grew up. When God introduced Himself at the burning bush, Moses knew God was the only true God. Our God is a fact. He always has been, and He always will be. We can count on our unchanging God.

The Mystery of the Name
(Exodus 3-4:13)

BIBLE LESSON

Before the Bible Lesson, hide clues 1-4 around the room *(page 127)*. Each clue relates to the Bible Lesson. Have kids scramble to find the clues before grabbing their Bibles and sitting down.

 INTRO

During ZOOM, we are beginning to answer the question "Who is God?" by ZOOMING in on different names of God. The Bible gives God a lot of different names that all mean different things, and each name gives us a small clue to the big picture of who God is. So far, we have learned that God is Creator, God is Enough, and God is Provider. Even with just those three clues, we can tell God is amazing and deserves our worship.

Today we are going to ZOOM in on another one of God's names.

 Who has CLUE #1?

Give the person who found Clue #1 a "decoder" (a piece of red cellophane). Let them read the first clue to the class. Clue #1 is: "'Yahweh' means 'I AM THAT I AM.' God is the self-existent One." (YAH-weh)

This clue might be a little confusing. Today we will learn about the name of God, I AM. Most people hear this name and wonder, "I am ... what? What is the end of that sentence?"

 Who has CLUE #2?

Give the person who found Clue #2 a "decoder" (a piece of red cellophane). Let them read the clue to the class. Clue #2 is: "Yahweh is sometimes written as the Hebrew word Jehovah."

God's name, Yahweh, can also be translated as the name Jehovah. Both names come from the same root word in Hebrew. The name Jehovah might sound familiar. We learned the name Jehovah-Jireh last time. Remember Jehovah-Jireh means "God is Provider." Literally, it means "I AM Provider." God is many things. There are many ways to end the sentence I AM. But sometimes, God finishes the sentence right there with I AM. He does not add anything else to His name. Let's see where this name of God can be found in the Bible.

 Who has CLUE #3?

Give the person who found Clue #3 a "decoder" (a piece of red cellophane). Let them read the clue to the class. Clue #3 is: "The Mystery of the Name, Exodus 3-4."

 # READ THE BIBLE

Open your Bibles to Exodus 3. **Read Exodus 3:1-6.**

Can you imagine how Moses must have felt when God spoke to him from a burning bush that was not actually burning? Moses saw this miracle, heard God's voice, and knew right away that God was special. He was holy. Moses knew God was different from everything else he had ever seen or known. From the bush, God told Moses that He had seen the Hebrews suffer in slavery. God wanted to set them free, and He wanted to use Moses as a part of His plan. God told Moses to tell Pharaoh to let His people go.

• How would you feel if God told you to tell Pharaoh to give up his slaves?

Let's see what Moses said. **Read Exodus 3:10-12.**

Moses thought God had picked the wrong man for the job. He felt like he was a nobody. He did not think he was able to do what God wanted him to do. God answered Moses by reminding him He would be with Moses the whole time.

Moses was not convinced. The Hebrews would think he was crazy. Besides, the Egyptians worshiped a lot of different gods. Which god should he tell the Hebrews had sent him?

Read Exodus 3:13-15.

Did you hear that? That's the name of God we are learning today. God is Yahweh, the I AM. Exodus 3:15 tells us this is God's name forever. God was telling Moses He wasn't just any "little g" god. He was, and is, the only God. All other gods are fake. Our God, Yahweh, is real. More than that, I AM will be God's name forever. He is the "Self-Existent One;" God does not change, get tired, or grow old. However God is now, we can be confident He will always be this way. For example, we know God is loving, so we can count on God to always be loving. He will not run out of love.

- What else do you know about God?

God's name, Yahweh, tells us God is who He is and will always be this way. God will always be strong. He will not run out of power. God will always be patient. He will not run out of patience.

In fact, God was very patient with Moses. Even after hearing God was the Great I AM, Moses still had questions about going to Egypt. Exodus 4 tells us Moses was worried the Hebrews would not believe God had sent him. God answered Moses by giving him the ability to do miracles. God gave Moses the ability to turn a staff into a snake and back into a staff again. He gave Moses the ability to give himself leprosy and heal himself again. He gave Moses the ability to turn water from the Nile River into blood.

But even after all of that, Moses was still nervous. **Read Exodus 4:10-12.**

Moses gave another excuse. He did not speak well. He stuttered when he spoke. God answered Moses by reminding him He was Elohim, the One who created his mouth. God knew exactly who Moses was and what he was able to do. God did not forget Moses stuttered. Moses had forgotten that the God he was speaking with was the I AM: the God who can do anything, the God who had promised to be with him as he went to Pharaoh in Egypt, the God who never changes, the God who could have rescued His people on His own, but chose to use Moses.

PRESENT THE GOSPEL

If you ever think you are not good enough to be used by God, remember Moses. He was nervous. He did not think he was good enough. Listen closely - God knows exactly how He made you. He made you on purpose and for a purpose. He knows you, loves you, and wants you to be part of His forever family.

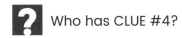 Who has CLUE #4?

Give the person who found Clue #4 a "decoder" (a piece of red cellophane). Let them read the clue to the class. Clue #4 is: "God loves you. John 3:16."

That's right! In fact, John 3:16 tells us God loved everyone in the world so much that He gave His only Son, Jesus. Jesus came to earth to take the punishment that you and I deserve for our wrong choices, our sins, even though He had never done anything wrong.

God knows you, and He has great plans. He wants you to be a part of His plans, to be a part of His adventure on this earth. But first, we have to choose to be His. ADMIT you have sinned. BELIEVE Jesus, God's Son, died on the cross for you and came back to life three days later. CHOOSE to belong to God. CHOOSE to put God in charge of your life from now on.

 # APPLICATION

Imagine what would have happened if Moses had been to afraid to obey God. Instead of leading an entire nation out of slavery and to the land God had promised them, Moses would still have been a shepherd. He never would have seen the amazing things God did to free His people. He would have missed seeing God's power during the ten plagues and the parting of the Red Sea. He never would have seen God's provision of manna and quail in the wilderness. He never would have gotten to spend time with God on the top of Mount Sinai.

Thankfully for Moses, he did choose to put God in charge. And because he did, each day he grew closer and closer to God. Moses became best friends with God. God wants to be best friends with you, too. He made you. He loves you. He wants you to be His. And because God is the I AM, He will never change.

PRAY

ACTIVITY 3 • THE GAME CHANGER

MATERIALS: Paper hole punch confetti, Cups, Marker

DIRECTIONS: *Before Class*, fill one cup three-quarters full with paper hole punches. Mark a line at the very top of the cup. Be sure there are not enough hole punches to reach the line at the top of the cup.

During Class, divide your class into two teams. Tell teams the object of the game is to collect as many hole punches as possible before time runs out. If a team can fill the cup up to the line, they will get bonus points.

Choose one team to play first. On your mark, throw the hole punches into the air. After a few seconds, pause the game. Tell kids they can now only use one hand to collect the punches. Resume the game. After about thirty seconds, stop the game and tally their progress.

Have everyone collect the hole punches again. On your mark, throw the hole punches again and let the second team try to collect. After a few seconds, tell the kids they cannot crawl on the ground. Only their feet can touch the floor, not their knees. Resume the game.

As you have time, play again, making more and more changes to the the game as the kids are playing.

 MAKE THE CONNECTION:
- Was this game fair? Why / why not?
- Was it even possible to earn the bonus points?

Today we learned God is Yahweh, the Great I AM. In other words, God is the self-existent One. Unlike the rules in our game, He never changes. And unlike our hole punches, God's ability never runs out. He will always be enough. He has no time limit. He never gets tired. He never goes back on a promise. He never gives up. **Hebrews 13:8 says, "Jesus Christ is the same yesterday and today and forever."** We can count on God.

ACTIVITY 4 • MEMORY VERSE

MATERIALS: Balloons, Balloon pumps, Small paper strips, Pen, Painters' tape

DIRECTIONS: *Before Class*, write the verse, one word at a time, on small strips of paper. Make as many sets as you plan to have teams in your class. *During Class*, give each team a set of verse strips, a balloon, and a balloon pump. On your mark, kids take turns inflating the balloon with the pump and aiming the balloon air at each paper strip to blow it past the painters' tape. The first team to get all of the strips across the line and in order wins. (Hint: the paper strips are easier to move if they have been wadded into balls.)

MAKE THE CONNECTION:

John 8:58 says, **"Jesus said to them, 'Truly, truly, I say to you, before Abraham was born, I AM.'"** Jesus was telling the people He was, and is, God. Before He came to earth as a baby, Jesus was with God in Heaven. Jesus is amazing, and one day everyone will know it. Our memory verse tells us one day, everyone will know that Jesus is God. They will all bow down to Him. In our game, the balloon kept running out of air, slowing down the process. Aren't you glad you serve an amazing God, the one true God who will never run out of energy, love, compassion, or care? Jesus is the same always. He is the I AM. We can count on Him, because He is God.

ALTERNATE MEMORY VERSE GAME: Bring several wind-up toys. Let kids race the toys across the room. When the toy reaches the finish line, hand the team one memory verse strip. The first team to correctly order the verse wins. Make the same connection. Even though the wind up toys kept running out of energy, we serve a God who will never get tired.

ACTIVITY 5 • SPELL IT OUT: YAHWEH

MATERIALS: YAHWEH papers *(pages 129, 131)*, Music, Music player

DIRECTIONS: Hand one paper to each player. If your class does not evenly split into groups of six, give some players two consecutive letters. Play music. Have kids walk around the room until the music stops. When the music stops, kids must get in groups of six to spell out the name Yahweh. When everyone has found a group, have the group state the meaning of the name Yahweh and one reason He deserves our worship..

 MAKE THE CONNECTION:

Who is God? God is many things, and all of them are good. Today we ZOOMED in on Yahweh, the name of God that tells us God is the I AM! God is self existent. He does not need anything. He has always been and He always will be. God is the answer to every problem. I AM all you need. I AM enough. I AM the answer. Moses was not enough, but the I AM was enough.

• What does that tell you about God?

• The name I AM is one of the most powerful names of God. How does God answer our problems with His name, I AM?

• What do you know about God so far? What does that tell you about who God will be in the future? *(He will be the same.)*

God is forever. He will never die or get tired. He will always be good. He will always be loving. He will always be God. He will never change. We can count on God.

Q: When was God born?

A: God was not born. He has always been, and He always will be. This is not a perfect example, but imagine God is like the author of a book. The author writes the book to happen in the 1800's, but the author was not actually born in the 1800's. He knows what happens in the beginning, the middle, and the end of the book. The author can change what happens, because he is the author. God is like the author. He created time. It's hard for us to imagine life without time, but that's how God lives. He was not born, and He will never grow old. It is a great thing to know God will always be there for you and for me!

Q: Why is "I AM" capitalized in the Bible?

A: Yahweh is the most holy name of God. The people who wrote down the Bible capitalized it to show this name of God is holy. In fact, many Jews will not even say the name Yahweh aloud. They treat this name of God as holy, special.

CLUE 5

JEHOVAH-RAPHA:
God is Healer.

MEMORY VERSE

"Therefore, God elevated him to the place of highest honor and gave him the name above all other names, that at the name of Jesus every knee should bow, in heaven and on earth and under the earth, and every tongue declare that Jesus Christ is Lord, to the glory of God the Father." Philippians 2:9-11

ZOOM!

Bible Lesson: The Mystery of the Mat and the Mud (Mark 2:1-13, John 9)

INVESTIGATIVE
SUPPLIES

ACTIVITY 1:

First Aid Kit Template *(pages 133-135, 137)*, Scissors,

Tape, Various art supplies

ACTIVITY 2:

Blindfolds, Markers, Paper (individual sheets or butcher paper)

BIBLE LESSON:

Clues *(page 139)*, Decoder (piece of red cellophane)

ACTIVITY 3:

Two old bed sheets or large towels

ACTIVITY 4:

Bandage cards *(pages 141, 143, 145, 147, 149)*

ACTIVITY 5:

JEHOVAH-RAPHA papers *(pages 151, 153)*,

Music, Music player

LEADER DEVOTION

Read Mark 2:1-13 and John 9.

In these passages, Jesus heals men from illness and from sin. In each instance, Jesus uses the ravages of a fallen world to bring glory to God the Father. He heals what has been broken, so God will be known. In Mark, a man's friends bring him to Jesus for healing. In John, Jesus seeks out a man, born blind, to affirm his innocence in his sickness and to heal him. Both times, Jesus healed inside and out. Most of us remember the times God brought healing in the Old Testament and the incredible stories of Jesus' healings in the New Testament. But what about the times He does not heal?

The name Jehovah-Rapha is deeply personal to me. Eighteen years ago, I was diagnosed with Lupus. To this day, I struggle to manage my pain and energy levels during flare ups. I have a disease with no known cure. But I know when there is hurt, I have a Healer. Like the many others waiting by the pool at Bethesda, in another of Jesus' many stories of healing in John 5, He may not choose to heal me on this earth. Instead, He uses my hurt to His glory.

Because God is my Healer, I can confidently continue doing what He calls me to do. For instance, it is not "doctor approved" attempting to learn the guitar while trying to manage joint pain in my hands; however, I knew God was calling me to lead worship with the guitar. Though there is pain in the offering, God is my Great Physician. Several years later, I am using the guitar to lead kids in worship, teaching them how to worship our awesome God. Because I have Lupus, I have witnessed Him work miracles, through my swollen hands, that no one else understands. As I continue to follow Him, He continues to give me the health I need to serve Him in the way He has called me to serve.

One day, when He calls me to other things, He may not provide the ability to serve Him in these ways. God may allow my disease to get worse. Still, I recognize God is the Giver of the health I have had, have currently, and will have in the future. He is my supernatural Sustainer. Because God is my Jehovah-Rapha, my heart has been healed through the sacrificial blood of Jesus Christ and one day, whether on earth or in Heaven, I will be healed physically as well.

As we learned last week, God is the I AM, not the I WAS. I'm sick, but He is still Healer. He heals today in miraculous ways all around the world. Do you need healing physically? Spiritually? God is Jehovah-Rapha. He has promised to heal all who are in Christ. Put your hope in the Great Physician, who made your body and soul.

WELCOME

ACTIVITY 1 • FIRST-AID KIT CRAFT

MATERIALS: First Aid Kit Template *(pages 133-135, 137)*, Scissors, Tape, Various art supplies

DIRECTIONS: Have kids cut out the template and fold it down the middle. Tape the sleeves to the insides of the kit. Allow kids to decorate the kit. Cut out the verse cards and place them inside the sleeves.

MAKE THE CONNECTION:

When you scrape your knees and elbows, you need a first-aid kit. Sometimes, we get hurt on the inside. When we are hurting inside (hurt feelings, sad, worried, etc.), the Bible is our first-aid kit. Today we will learn God is our Healer. He can heal us on the outside and the inside, too.

ACTIVITY 2 • BLINDFOLDED ART

MATERIALS: Blindfolds, Markers, Paper (individual sheets or butcher paper)

DIRECTIONS: Hand out paper and markers, then blindfold everyone in your class. With blindfolds on, tell kids to draw a house with a family standing outside. You can make the drawing as easy or as complicated as you like. Let kids take off the blindfolds to see their drawings. Play again, but this time choose one person to be "it." If "it" tags you while you draw, you can take off your blindfold and finish drawing.

MAKE THE CONNECTION:

Your drawings looked much better when you were not blindfolded. Today we are ZOOMING in on the fact that God is our Healer. Many people in this world are sick. Some cannot see. God promises He will heal all of the diseases of everyone who believes in Jesus (Psalm 103:1-3). In our second game, not all of you were able to take off the blindfolds right away. Some of you had to wait. In the same way, God does not promise us He will always heal our bodies right away on this earth. Sometimes we have to wait until Heaven. Either way, God, our Healer, promises that one day, everyone who believes in Him will be healed. That is good news!

BIBLE LESSON

Before the Bible Lesson, hide clues 1-5 around the room *(page 139)*. Each clue relates to the Bible Lesson. Have kids scramble to find the clues before grabbing their Bibles and sitting down.

 ## INTRO

During ZOOM, we are beginning to answer the question "Who is God?" by ZOOMING in on the different names of God. The Bible gives God a lot of different names that all mean different things. Each name gives us a small clue to the big picture of who God is.

Today we are going to ZOOM in on another one of God's names.

 Who has CLUE #1?

Give the person who found Clue #1 a "decoder" (a piece of red cellophane). Let them read the first clue to the class. Clue #1 is: "'Jehovah-Rapha' means 'God is Healer.'" (Ji-hoh-vuh - Rah-fah)

God is our Healer. Raise your hand if you have ever been sick. Raise your hand if you have ever scraped your knees or elbows. Raise your hand if you have ever broken a bone. Raise your hand if you have ever gone to the doctor for a check-up. Raise your hand if you have ever had hurt feelings. Raise your hand if you have ever needed to be forgiven. Raise your hand if you have ever felt worried or afraid.

Wow! It looks like everyone in this class needs a healer. Sometimes we need God to heal our bodies from sickness or other hurts. Other times, we need God to heal our hearts. What kind of Healer is God? Do you think He can heal our bodies? What about our hearts? Do you think He can heal both?

The best place to look for the answer to these questions is the Bible. Where should we look?

 Who has CLUE #2?

Give the person who found Clue #2 a "decoder" (a piece of red cellophane). Let them read the clue to the class. Clue #2 is: "'The Mystery of the Mat. Mark 2:1-13."

READ THE BIBLE

Read Mark 2:1-5.
People came from all over to see Jesus. They knew Jesus could heal diseases. One day, four men brought a paralyzed friend to Jesus.

- Why do you think they brought the paralyzed man to Jesus? *(to be healed, to be able to walk)*
- Do you think they were surprised, when Jesus forgave his sins?

Jesus saw the man needed to be healed on the outside, but He understood that the paralyzed man had bigger problems than not being able to walk.

PRESENT THE GOSPEL

 Who has CLUE #3?

Give the person who found Clue #3 a "decoder" (a piece of red cellophane). Let them read the clue to the class. Clue #3 is: "Jesus heals our hearts from sin."

Sin is a big problem that each of us has. The Bible says we all have sinned. We have chosen to do wrong, to do things our way instead of God's way. This is a big problem, because the punishment for sin is death and separation from our God, who loves us. Thankfully, God is Jehovah-Rapha. He is the God who heals. He is God who heals our hearts from sin. Jesus came to earth, lived a perfect life, then died on the cross. He chose to take the punishment that we deserved for our wrong choices. Jesus came back to life three days later. Now, we can be healed from the sickness of sin. We can be forgiven for our wrong choices and become a part of God's forever family. ADMIT you have sinned. BELIEVE that Jesus took the punishment you deserved, when He chose to die on the cross. Praise Him for coming back to life! CHOOSE to put Jesus in charge of your life. Make Him the Lord, the Boss, of your life from now on. Jesus will heal you from the inside out.

READ THE BIBLE

The people did not understand that Jesus is God. When He forgave the man's sins, the people started to think bad things about Jesus. They did not understand that Jesus can heal our hearts from sin. To prove He really was God's perfect Son, Jesus did something amazing.

Read Mark 2:10-12.
Jesus healed the man's body, too. God has the power to heal our hearts from sin, and He has the power to heal our outside bodies. Throughout the Bible, there are many stories of God's healing power. In the Old Testament, God healed the Israelites in the desert many times. He healed King Hezekiah, giving him a long life. In the New Testament, Jesus healed many people, including the paralyzed man whose friends brought him to Jesus for healing.

What story of God's amazing, healing power should we hear next?

 Who has CLUE #4?

Give the person who found Clue #4 a "decoder" (a piece of red cellophane). Let them read the clue to the class. Clue #4 is: "'The Mystery of the Mud. John 9."

Read John 9:1-5.
When the disciples saw the man who was born blind, they thought he had sinned, and God's punishment for his sin was blindness. Jesus explained his blindness was not a consequence of sin. People do not always get sick because they sinned. God is not punishing you every time you get a cold. Sometimes we get sick as a result of our disobedience. For example, if your parents told you not to play in the cold rain, and you disobeyed them, you might get sick. Disobeying your parents might put you in a situation where you could get sick. This does not mean every person who is sick did something wrong.

Being sick is no fun at all, but God can use even the not-fun things in this world to share the Good News. Jesus explained that God was going to use this man's blindness to bring Him glory, to make God famous for the amazing things He does on the earth.

Read John 9:6-7.
Jesus healed the man. He could see for the first time in his life. That is amazing! Unfortunately, the Bible tells us people were not very happy about the miracle Jesus had done. Many people did not want to believe in Jesus. They said the man who had been healed was lying. When the man told the story of how Jesus had healed him, the other Jews became very angry. They told him he could not come back to the synagogue anymore.

Read John 9:35-38.
Jesus found the man and told him He was really God's Son, God's plan to save the world from sin. Again, Jesus not only healed this man's blindness, but also healed his hurting heart. Jesus accepted the man as one of His disciples, as one of His friends when all of the man's other friends, and even his own family, turned their backs on him.

 # APPLICATION

Jehovah-Rapha means God is our Healer. He can heal us on the outside, and He can heal the inside of our hearts. We serve an amazing God!

 Who has CLUE #5?

Give the person who found Clue #5 a "decoder" (a piece of red cellophane). Let them read the clue to the class. Clue #5 is: "Psalm 103:1-3."

Read Psalm 103:1-3.
One day, whether here on earth or in Heaven, God will heal ALL of His children's diseases. God promises to heal everyone who believes in Jesus as their Lord, their Boss. That is amazing!

God is our Healer. When you hurt on the outside or on the inside of your heart, pray. Talk to God about your hurts. Ask Him to heal you, and know God is able to do everything you ask of Him. His plans are perfect, and He will heal everyone who belongs to Him. God is our Healer.

PRAY

Pray with your class. You can let kids take turns praying for people who are sick. Remind them to pray for people whose hearts are in need of healing as well.

God is Healer.

JEHOVAH-RAPHA

ACTIVITY 3 • TAKE YOUR MAT RELAY

MATERIALS: Two old bed sheets or large towels

DIRECTIONS: Divide your class into two teams. Be sure everyone on each team has a partner. Give each team an old bed sheet or a large towel. On your mark, the first set of partners runs the relay. One person rides on the towel or sheet, while the other drags them to the opposite side of the wall. Both run back to hand the sheet or towel to the next pair on their team. The first team to completely finish wins.

MAKE THE CONNECTION:

The paralyzed man's friends brought him to Jesus for healing. Jesus healed the man's heart from sin and his body from being paralyzed. We can bring our friends to God for healing, too. We can pray, asking God to heal our friends and family. Our God is strong. He has the power to heal our outside bodies – He made them, after all! God also has the power to heal our hearts from sin. Jesus took our punishment on the cross, so we could be forgiven for every wrong choice we ever make. God can also heal our hearts from hurt. God is our Healer. We can bring any problem we have to Him, because He is strong enough to heal every situation.

ACTIVITY 4 • MEMORY VERSE

MATERIALS: Bandage cards *(pages 141, 143, 145, 147, 149)*

DIRECTIONS: *Before Class*, make several sets of the bandage cards, and cut them out. *During Class*, review the verse with your group. Divide your class into as many groups as you have sets of cards. Shuffle each set of cards, and hand them out to the groups. On your mark, groups race to put the verse in order. The first team to correctly order the verse and say it out loud wins.

"Therefore, God elevated him to the place of highest honor and gave him the name above all other names, that at the name of Jesus every knee should bow, in heaven and on earth and under the earth, and every tongue declare that Jesus Christ is Lord, to the glory of God the Father." Philippians 2:9-11

MAKE THE CONNECTION:

One day, everyone will finally understand that Jesus is God. They will bow down to Him, because He deserves our worship. I don't want to wait that long to worship God. I want to start worshiping Him now!

With an attitude of worship, review the names of God you have already learned. Give each name as a reason God deserves our worship.

ACTIVITY 5 • SPELL IT OUT: JEHOVAH-RAPHA

MATERIALS: JEHOVAH-RAPHA papers *(pages 151, 153)*, Music, Music player

DIRECTIONS: Hand one paper to each player. If your group does not evenly split into groups of six, give some players two consecutive letters. Play music. Have kids walk around the room until the music stops. When the music stops, kids must get in groups of six to spell out the name Jehovah-Rapha. When everyone has found a group, have the group state the meaning of the name Jehovah-Rapha and one story of God's healing (from the Bible or current day). Start the music again. Have kids get in different groups each time you stop the music.

MAKE THE CONNECTION:

Who is God? God is many things, and all of them are good. Today we ZOOMED in on Jehovah-Rapha, the name of God that tells us God is our Healer. He heals our outside bodies, and He heals our hearts.

- What does that tell you about God?
- How does God heal us?
- How has Jesus healed our hearts from sin?

God loves us very much. He heals our outside bodies and the inside of our hearts.

Q: Why didn't God heal my grandma?

A: God promises to heal everyone who believes in Him. Sometimes, God heals our outside bodies on earth. Other times, God chooses to heal our bodies in Heaven. Either way, God has a plan to heal everyone who believes in Him. One day, we all will be healed. The Bible says God will wipe every tear from our eyes. There will be no more pain. Thank the Lord He wants, and can, accomplish those good things for us!

Q: Why does God allow people to be sick?

A: When God made the world, no one was sick. When people sinned, sickness came into the world. That does NOT mean every person who is sick has done something wrong. It just means that sin hurts everyone. Thankfully, this world is not our forever home. If you believe in Jesus, your forever home is Heaven. There is no sickness in Heaven. Until Heaven, God uses even the not-so-great things on earth, like sickness, to tell people and teach people about Him. That way, even more people will know Him. Even more people will get to live in Heaven with God!

ADONAI:
God is Lord.

....

MEMORY VERSE

"Therefore, God elevated him to the place of highest honor and gave him the name above all other names, that at the name of Jesus every knee should bow, in heaven and on earth and under the earth, and every tongue declare that Jesus Christ is Lord, to the glory of God the Father." Philippians 2:9-11

?

Bible Lesson: The Mystery of
the Throne (Isaiah 6:1-8)

INVESTIGATIVE
SUPPLIES

ACTIVITY 1:

Building materials (blocks, modeling dough,

index cards with tape, pipe cleaners, etc.)

ACTIVITY 2:

None

BIBLE LESSON:

Clues *(page 155)*, Decoder (piece of red cellophane)

ACTIVITY 3:

Paper, Markers

ACTIVITY 4:

None

ACTIVITY 5:

ADONAI papers *(pages 157, 159)*, Music, Music player

ZO?M!

LEADER DEVOTION

Read Isaiah 6:1-8.

King Uzziah, a good and God-fearing king of Judah, had reigned for fifty-two years. Under Uzziah's reign, Judah had prospered and lived with a certain degree of stability. When a king died, the people became uncertain about their future. Would the new king be as stable as Uzziah? Would the king fear God or turn to idols? Would the country be safe under the new king's protection? In this time of uncertainty, the year that King Uzziah died, God showed Himself to Isaiah as Adonai, Master, the King of kings.

In the throne room of God, Isaiah had no question about who was in charge. He saw God's holiness, recognized his sin, and, being forgiven of his sins, volunteered to be subject to God as his Master. Isaiah committed to go where his Master sent him and to do what his Master told him to do. The new king was not to be Isaiah's true Master, God was. Because God was his Master, he did not have to worry. He could trust that the unchanging, omnipotent, omniscient, and omnipresent God had everything under control. He could trust that no matter what happened under the new earthly king of Judah, God was still in charge.

In the same way, God invites us into His presence, where we become painfully aware of our sins and God's holiness. Through Christ, our sins are forgiven, and He asks us to recognize the fact of His Lordship. To declare Christ as Lord is to deny all other masters in our lives. There is only one Adonai. What or whom have you allowed to take mastery over you; to sway your thoughts, sense of identity and purpose, words, and actions?

Mastery comes in many forms. For some, substance abuse takes a position of lordship over their lives, be it with recreational drugs, alcohol, or food. Others allow people to take lordship over them, determining their identities and self-worth. For some of us, mastery can manifest itself in a thirst for control, the thirst to be our own master. We mistakenly think if we can master the people, schedules, clothes, transportation, food, etc., around us, there will be peace. However, in our efforts to guarantee peace, we have taken a role that was not intended to be ours. We have taken the role of "master."

Let go of the illusion of control in your life. Acknowledge God alone as your Lord and Master. Give Him every area of your life, every day, and rest in the fact that He is the unchanging King of kings. He is in control, and that is a good thing.

WELCOME

ACTIVITY 1 • MASTER BUILDER

MATERIALS: Building materials (blocks, modeling dough, index cards with tape, pipe cleaners, etc.)

DIRECTIONS: Split your class into several smaller groups, and distribute the building materials. On your mark, groups begin to build exactly what you tell them to build. Each group who builds what you tell them to build gets a point. Give the groups several different things to build before making the connection. (Examples of things to build: house, zoo, car, space ship, etc.)

MAKE THE CONNECTION:

Your teams did a great job building the things I told you to build. At construction sites, there is always someone who knows the building plan and is in charge. That person tells everyone else what to build and how to build it.

• What might happen if people did not listen to the person in charge?

Today we will learn God is in charge. He is the Master, the Lord, the Boss, of everything. We should listen to Him and obey Him.

ACTIVITY 2 • WHO'S IN CHARGE HERE?!

MATERIALS: None

DIRECTIONS: Play a game of "Simon Says" with a twist. Choose two different people to be "Simon" at the same time. Both leaders must give commands simultaneously, forcing players to choose which Simon they will follow. After playing a few rounds like this, make the connection and play once more with only one Simon.

MAKE THE CONNECTION:

"Simon Says" does not work with two Simons. You could not obey both Simons all of the time. At some point in the game, you had to choose which Simon you were going to follow. You had to choose which Simon was in charge of you during the game. Today we are learning God is in charge. He is the Lord, the Boss, the Master. Just like in the game, it does not work to say we follow God and something else. There is only one Lord, and that is God!

The Mystery of the Throne
(Isaiah 6:1-8)

BIBLE LESSON

Before the Bible Lesson, hide clues 1-4 around the room *(page 155)*. Each clue relates to the Bible Lesson. Have kids scramble to find the clues before grabbing their Bibles and sitting down.

▶ INTRO

During ZOOM, we are beginning to answer the question "Who is God?" by ZOOMING in on a few of the different names of God. The Bible gives God a lot of different names that all mean different things. Each name gives us a small clue to the big picture of who God is.

Today we are going to ZOOM in on another one of God's names.

 Who has CLUE #1?

Give the person who found Clue #1 a "decoder" (a piece of red cellophane). Let them read the first clue to the class. Clue #1 is: "'Adonai means 'Lord.'" (Ah-don-eye)

We are learning the name of God, Adonai. Adonai means Lord, or Boss. The Bible uses this name for God a lot. Let's see where we are going to look for Adonai in the Bible.

 Who has CLUE #2?

Give the person who found Clue #2 a "decoder" (a piece of red cellophane). Let them read the clue to the class. Clue #2 is: "The Mystery of the Throne. Isaiah 6:1-8."

The book of Isaiah is in the Old Testament, a few books after Psalms. Isaiah, the author of the book, was a prophet. That means he listened to God and told the people what God said. In Isaiah 6, Isaiah tells us about a vision he had from God in a very uncertain time in his life.

READ THE BIBLE

Read Isaiah 6:1.

- What did Isaiah see?
- Who had just died?

King Uzziah, a very good king of Judah, had just died. Uzziah had been in charge of Judah for fifty-two years. That is a long time! While he was king, Judah had strong armies and a good economy. Isaiah felt safe under King Uzziah's leadership. Now that Uzziah was dead, a new king was going to be on the throne. No one knew what kind of king he would be.

We don't have kings, but we can still identify with the way Isaiah must have felt. Have you ever felt nervous on the first day of school because you were worried about meeting your new teacher? It can be scary meeting a new person who is going to be in charge. In this time when Isaiah was worried about the new king, God gave Isaiah a vision of Himself as King in the throne room of Heaven.

ACTIVITY 3 • DRAW IT

MATERIALS: Paper, Markers

DIRECTIONS: Pass out blank sheets of paper and markers to the class. As you read Isaiah 6:1-8, have the kids draw what they imagine Isaiah saw.

I'm going to slowly read Isaiah 6:1-4. As I read, use your imagination to draw a picture of what Isaiah saw.

Read Isaiah 6:1-4 slowly, stopping to allow kids to draw the scene in Heaven.

 # READ THE BIBLE

When Isaiah saw God in His throne room, he knew right away God was in charge. Isaiah called God "Adonai," Lord. He knew God was the King of everything and always would be the King.

Imagine seeing God on His throne. What do you think you would do? How would you react?

 Who has CLUE #3?

Give the person who found Clue #3 a "decoder" (a piece of red cellophane). Let them read the clue to the class. Clue #3 is: "'Holy' means 'set apart.' God is set apart, because He has no sin in Him."

Read Isaiah 6:5.

Isaiah saw how amazing God is and instantly realized he did not deserve to be there. God has no sin. God is holy. But Isaiah had sinned. He had said things he shouldn't have, and he knew he was in trouble.

Read Isaiah 6:6-7.

 Who has CLUE #4?

Give the person who found Clue #4 a "decoder" (a piece of red cellophane). Let them read the clue to the class. Clue #4 is: "'Atoned for' means 'paid for.' The punishment for Isaiah's sin had been paid."

 # PRESENT THE GOSPEL

God forgave Isaiah for his sin, and Isaiah was allowed to stay in the throne room with God. The Bible tells us we all have sinned. Whether we have said things we shouldn't have like Isaiah, or sinned in some other way, we all have chosen to do wrong things. Those wrong things keep us from God. Thankfully, God loves us so much He sent Jesus to "atone," or pay the price, for our sins. Jesus never sinned, but He took the punishment for all of our sins, when He died on the cross. Jesus did not stay dead, though! Miraculously, Jesus came back to life three days later!

Isaiah was very sorry for the wrong choices he had made and was forgiven for his sins. He understood God was his Lord, his Adonai, his Boss forever. Because of that, God allowed him to be in the throne room with Him. God even allowed him to be a part of the amazing things He was doing in the world.

Have you made Jesus your Adonai, your Boss? Tell God you are very sorry for the wrong choices you have made. Ask Him to forgive you. Thank Him for sending Jesus to take your punishment for you on the cross. Thank Him for amazingly coming back to life three days later. Then tell Jesus you choose to put Him in charge of your life from now on. Choose to make Him your Boss, your Lord, your Adonai. When we put Jesus in charge, God brings us into His forever family. That is amazing!

 ## APPLICATION

Read Isaiah 6:8.

After being forgiven for his sins, Isaiah was excited to do anything his Lord and Master wanted him to do. God gave Isaiah the special job of telling the people in Judah things they did not want to hear. Isaiah told the people to stop sinning and to turn to God, but they did not listen to him. Even though the people did not listen, Isaiah never gave up. He always obeyed his Adonai, God, and trusted that God had a plan.

Isaiah made God his Boss every day of his life, and so should we. When we decide to put Jesus in charge, it is more than a one-time decision. Making Jesus your Boss is a lifestyle, an ongoing relationship with the King of kings. Like Isaiah, we can make Jesus our Boss and get excited to do anything God, our Lord, wants us to do.

PRAY

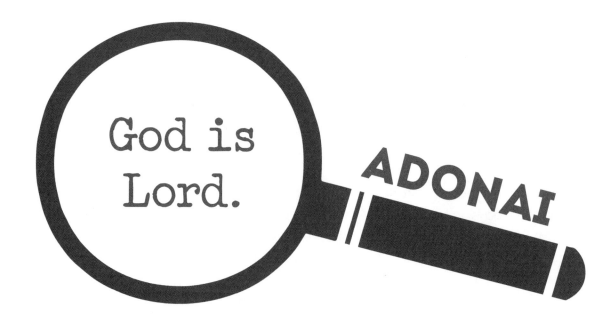

God is Lord.

ADONAI

ACTIVITY 4 · MEMORY VERSE

MATERIALS: None

DIRECTIONS: Review the memory verse with your class. Make motions to help everyone remember the key words and phrases.

"Therefore, God elevated him to the place of highest honor and gave him the name above all other names, that at the name of Jesus every knee should bow, in heaven and on earth and under the earth, and every tongue declare that Jesus Christ is Lord, to the glory of God the Father." Philippians 2:9-11

MAKE THE CONNECTION:

" **... and every tongue declare that Jesus Christ is Lord ...** " One day, everyone will know that God is Adonai. Whether or not they chose to believe in God in this life, one day everyone will know the truth. God is in charge. He is the King of kings, the Lord of lords. He is the Boss of all bosses, and He loves us all very, very much. We have learned so much about God and STILL we have not learned everything there is to know about our awesome God. Our God is absolutely amazing! Let's take time now to worship Him together.

With an attitude of worship, review the names of God you have already learned. Let kids give each name as a reason God deserves our worship.

ACTIVITY 5 • SPELL IT OUT: ADONAI

MATERIALS: ADONAI papers *(pages 157, 159)*, Music, Music player

DIRECTIONS: Hand one paper to each player. If your group does not evenly split into groups of six, give some players two consecutive letters. Play music. Have kids walk around the room until the music stops. When the music stops, kids must get in groups of six to spell out the name Adonai. When everyone has found a group, have the group state the meaning of the name Adonai and one reason they are thankful God is in charge. Start the music again. Have kids get in different groups each time you stop the music.

MAKE THE CONNECTION:

Who is God? God is many things, and all of them are good. Today we ZOOMED in on Adonai, the name of God that tells us God is our Lord. He is in charge.

- What does that tell you about God?
- What does it mean to make Jesus the Boss of your life?
- Is putting Jesus in charge a one-time thing, or is it a choice you make every day? Explain your answer.

God is Adonai. He is the Master. He is the Lord, the Boss, of everything. He is a good God, and we can trust that even when hard times come, God is in charge. He loves us and will take care of us.

Q: If God is in charge, why do bad things happen?

A: Imagine you programmed a robot to say "I love you" every time you flip the switch on. Would the robot really love you? Of course not! God did not make us to be robots. He gave us a choice. We can choose to love Him or not. When we choose to disobey God, that is called sin. Sin has consequences. Sometimes, bad things happen because of the sins we have committed. For example, you might be grounded, because you disobeyed your parents. Being grounded is a bad thing that happened because of your sin.

Other times, bad things happen because of someone else's sin (someone robs you, etc.). And still other things happen, because this whole world has sin and is waiting for Heaven (bad weather, sickness, etc.). The important thing to remember is that God is still in charge, when bad things happen. He uses the bad things that happen to do good things in His children's lives (learning to trust Him more in a trial, etc.). God is in charge, and one day He will come back.

ZOOM!

APPENDIX

Reproducible Pages

"THEREFORE, GOD ELEVATED HIM

TO THE PLACE OF HIGHEST HONOR

AND GAVE HIM THE NAME

ABOVE ALL OTHER NAMES..."

PHILIPPIANS 2:9

ELOHIM: God is Creator.

CLUE 1

CLUE 2

CLUE 3

CLUE 4

CLUE 5

ELOHIM: God is Creator.

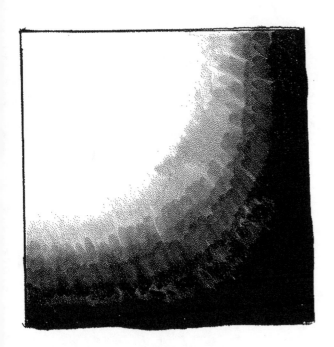

DAY 1: GOD CREATED LIGHT.

DAY 2: GOD CREATED THE SKY.

DAY 3: GOD CREATED DRY LAND.

DAY 3: GOD CREATED PLANTS.

ELOHIM: God is Creator.

DAY 4: GOD CREATED THE SUN.

DAY 4: GOD CREATED THE STARS.

DAY 4: GOD CREATED THE MOON.

DAY 4: GOD CREATED SEA CREATURES.

ELOHIM: God is Creator.

DAY 5: GOD CREATED BIRDS.

DAY 6: GOD CREATED ANIMALS.

DAY 6: GOD CREATED PEOPLE.

DAY 7: GOD RESTED.

CLUE 1

CLUE 2

CLUE 3

CLUE 4

CLUE 5

CLUE 6

EL SHADDAI: God is Enough.

ZO?M! CLUE **1**

ZO?M! CLUE **2**

ZO?M! CLUE **3**

ZO?M! CLUE **4**

ZO?M! CLUE **5**

CLUE 1

CLUE 2

CLUE 3

CLUE 4

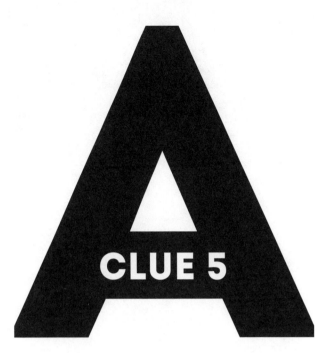

CLUE 5

CLUE 6

CLUE 7

CLUE 8

CLUE 9

WHAT NAME OF GOD MEANS "GOD IS PROVIDER"? COLOR TO FIND OUT!
1-BLUE, 2-GREEN, 3-YELLOW, 4-RED OR MAKE UP YOUR OWN COLOR CHART!

©28nineteen

JEHOVAH-JIREH: God is Provider.

CLUE 1

CLUE 2

CLUE 3

CLUE 4

CLUE 5

JEHOVAH-

CLUE 1

CLUE 2

CLUE 3

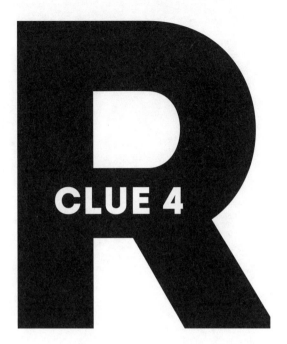

R CLUE 4

E CLUE 5

H CLUE 6

SAY THIS TO THE PEOPLE ISRAEL: TELL THEM

YAHWEH,

THE GOD OF YOUR ANCESTORS - THE GOD OF ABRAHAM, ISAAC, AND JACOB -
HAS SENT ME TO YOU. THIS IS MY ETERNAL NAME, MY NAME TO REMEMBER
FOR ALL GENERATIONS."   EXODUS 3:15

FACT OR FICTION?

PRETZELS WERE INVENTED BY MONKS TO LOOK LIKE ARMS FOLDED IN PRAYER.

FACT!

©28nineteen

FACT OR FICTION?

THE PEANUT IS A NUT.

FICTION!
THE PEANUT IS A MEMBER OF THE LEGUME FAMILY.

©28nineteen

FACT OR FICTION?

ALL FISH HAVE SCALES.

FICTION!
CATFISH, FOR EXAMPLE, DO NOT HAVE SCALES.

©28nineteen

FACT OR FICTION?

THE OSTRICH CAN RUN UP TO 40 MILES PER HOUR.

FACT!

©28nineteen

FACT OR FICTION?

THE KAGU IS A BIRD THAT CAN'T FLY AND BARKS LIKE A DOG.

FACT!

©28nineteen

FACT OR FICTION?

THE HUMAN BODY HAS OVER 300 BONES!

FICTION!
THE HUMAN BODY HAS 206 BONES.

©28nineteen

FACT OR FICTION?

THE WORD DINOSAUR MEANS "GREAT LIZARD".

FACT!

©28nineteen

FACT OR FICTION?

MILLIPEDES HAVE ONE THOUSAND LEGS.

FICTION!
THE MAXIMUM NUMBER OF LEGS IS JUST OVER 200.

©28nineteen

FACT OR FICTION?

FIDDLEHEAD IS THE NAME OF A GREEN VEGETABLE EATEN IN CANADA.

FACT!

©28nineteen

FACT OR FICTION?

TOMATOES ARE VEGETABLES.

FICTION!
TOMATOES ARE CLASSIFIED AS FRUITS.

©28nineteen

FACT OR FICTION?

YOUR BRAIN WEIGHS TWICE AS MUCH AS YOUR HEART.

FICTION!
YOUR BRAIN WEIGHS 3 TIMES AS MUCH AS YOUR HEART.

©28nineteen

FACT OR FICTION?

SHARKS CANNOT SWIM BACKWARDS.

FACT!

©28nineteen

FACT OR FICTION?

OUR BODIES ARE MORE THAN HALF WATER.

FACT!

©28nineteen

FACT OR FICTION?

THUNDER HAPPENS AFTER LIGHTNING STRIKES.

FICTION!
THEY HAPPEN AT THE SAME TIME, BUT LIGHT TRAVELS FASTER THAN SOUND.

©28nineteen

FACT OR FICTION?

THERE ARE MORE THAN 5 MILLION SHEEP IN WALES.

FACT!

©28nineteen

FACT OR FICTION?

THERE ARE ONLY 5 LAKES IN SWITZERLAND.

FICTION!
THERE ARE OVER A THOUSAND LAKES IN SWITZERLAND.

©28nineteen

YAHWEH: God is I AM.

ZO?M! CLUE 1

ZO?M! CLUE 2

ZO?M! CLUE 3

ZO?M! CLUE 4

127

©28nineteen

CLUE 1

©28nineteen

CLUE 2

©28nineteen

CLUE 3

©28nineteen

CLUE 4

©28nineteen

CLUE 5

CLUE 6

GOD IS MY HEALER

FIRST-AID KIT

133

134

GOD IS MY HEALER!

GOD IS MY HEALER!

WHEN I'M ...
WORRIED

PHILIPPIANS 4:6-7

"Don't worry about anything; instead, pray about everything. Tell God what you need, and thank him for all he has done. Then you will experience God's peace, which exceeds anything we can understand. His peace will guard your hearts and minds as you live in Christ Jesus."

See also: Matthew 6:25-34.

WHEN I'M ...
AFRAID

PSALM 56:3-4

"But when I am afraid, I will put my trust in you. I praise God for what he has promised. I trust in God, so why should I be afraid? What can mere mortals do to me?"

See also: Psalm 23.

WHEN I'M ... SAD

PSALM 40:1-3

"I waited patiently for the Lord to help me ... He lifted me out of the pit of despair ... He has given me a new song to sing, a hymn of praise to our God. Many will see what he has done and be amazed. They will put their trust in the Lord."

See also: **John 14:1-2.**

WHEN I'M ... TIRED

ISAIAH 40:30-31

"Even youths will become weak and tired, and young men will fall in exhaustion. But those who trust in the Lord will find new strength. They will soar high on wings like eagles. They will run and not grow weary. They will walk and not faint."

See also: **Psalm 121.**

WHEN I HAVE SINNED

1 JOHN 1:9

"But if we confess our sins to him, he is faithful and just to forgive us our sins and to cleanse us from all wickedness."

See also: **Psalm 51.**

WHEN I'M ... LONELY

JOSHUA 1:9

"This is my command — be strong and courageous! Do not be afraid or discouraged. For the Lord your God is with you wherever you go."

See also: **Matthew 28:19-20.**

JEHOVAH-RAPHA: God is Healer.

ZOOM! CLUE 1

ZOOM! CLUE 2

ZOOM! CLUE 3

ZOOM! CLUE 4

ZOOM! CLUE 5

"THEREFORE,

GOD ELEVATED

HIM TO THE

PLACE OF

HIGHEST HONOR

AND GAVE

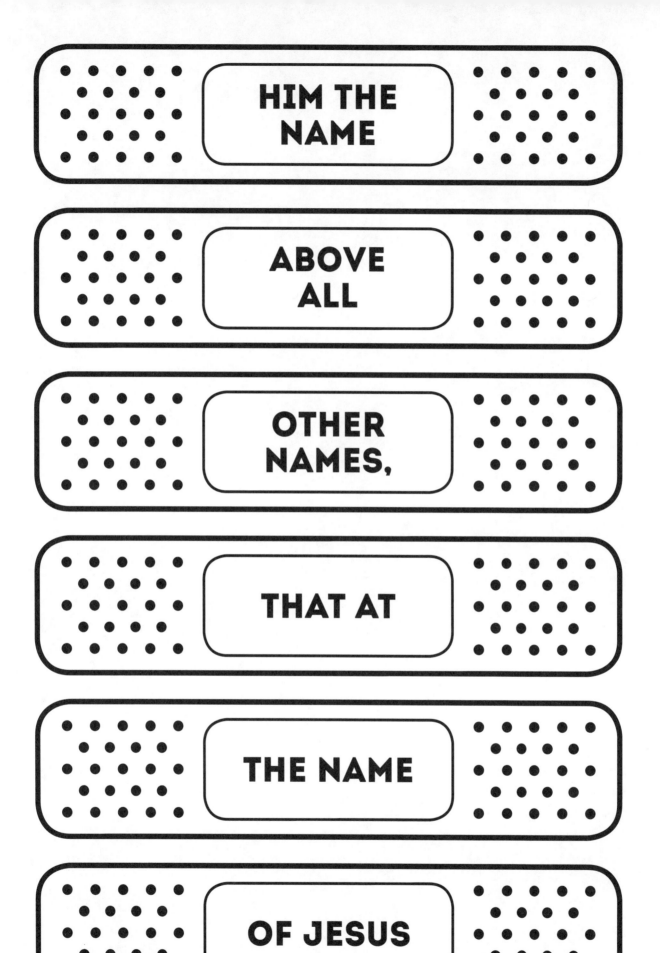

HIM THE
NAME

ABOVE
ALL

OTHER
NAMES,

THAT AT

THE NAME

OF JESUS

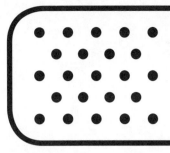 **EVERY KNEE**

 **SHOULD BOW,**

 **IN HEAVEN**

 **AND ON EARTH**

 **AND UNDER**

 **THE EARTH,**

AND EVERY

TONGUE

DECLARE

THAT JESUS

CHRIST IS

LORD, TO

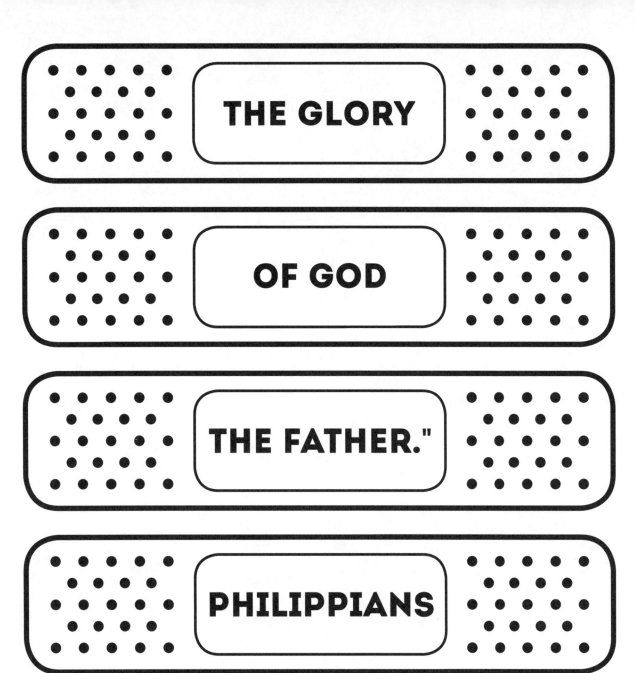

THE GLORY

OF GOD

THE FATHER."

PHILIPPIANS

2:9-11

149

JEHOVAH-

CLUE 1

CLUE 2

CLUE 3

P

CLUE 4

H

CLUE 5

A

CLUE 6

ADONAI: God is Lord.

CLUE 1

CLUE 2

CLUE 3

157

CLUE 4

CLUE 5

CLUE 6

ZO?M!

WHO IS GOD?

In ZOOM, we begin to answer that question by ZOOMING in on the different names of God. The Bible gives God various names that all mean different things. Each name gives us a small clue to the big picture of who God is. Junior detectives search for clues to catch the Puzzler and learn more about their benefactor, the mysterious Detective Zoom.

Enjoy the whole series!

Lower Elementary Leader Guide
ISBN 9781628628845

Take Home Resources
ISBN 9781628628890

Upper Elementary Leader Guide
ISBN 9781628628852

Children's Worship Program Guide
ISBN 9781628628876

www.28nineteencurriculum.com